Dreaming of
Our Better Selves

Dreaming of
Our Better Selves

Marion Tracy

Marion Tracy

Vanguard*Editions*

First published in the United Kingdom in 2016 by
Vanguard_Editions_
Flat 5
32a Camberwell Grove
London SE5 8RE

richardskinner.weebly.com

ISBN 978-1-84861-495-6

Copyright © Marion Tracy, 2016.

The right of Marion Tracy to be identified as the author of the work included in this volume has been asserted by her in accordance with the Copyrights, Designs and Patents Act of 1988. All rights reserved.

Cover photo © Bruno Novelli, 2016.

16 / 200

Contents

I

Stones	13
Mayan Sacrifice	14
Young girl with a tree in her brain	15
Virtual	16
The Beginning	17
Alien	18
Human	20
Grammatical second person talks back	21
How does the body lie?	22
Lady Macbeth	23
Malvolio	24
Pictures placed on high shelves in hospitals	25
Circular Breathing	27
Blog of the Ninth Lady, Stanton Moor	29

II — The Dreamer

Traffic	33
The Sleeper	34
Snowing	35
Fetch	36
Chicken	37
Dusk	38
La mer	39
Normality	40
Oil Spill	41
Banshee	42
Full Hunger Moon	43
Hearing Voices	44
The Wreath	45
Alteration	46

III

Recognition	51
Living Statues	52
Nest	55
Blind Mirror	56
Hotel Room	57
The Misadventures of her Purse	58
Moths	60
Ekphrastic	61
Mr and Mrs Death	62
Black Ice	63
Boundaries	64
Sense of everything	65
On the last day	66
The Spoiler	67

Acknowledgements

Acknowledgements are due to the editors of the following publications in which some of these poems first appeared. *14 Magazine, Artemis, Blue Dog* (Australia), *Iota, Mslexia, The North, Obsessed with Pipework, Poetry Review, Poetry Wales, The Rialto, Stand* and *Under the Radar*.

Also in the anthology *Peloton* (Templar Press). 'Pictures placed on high shelves in hospitals' was commended in the *Mslexia* Competition 2009. 'Alien' was longlisted in the National Poetry Competition 2012. 'Stones' was the Poem of the Year 2015/16 at the Second Light organization. 'Dusk' was runner up in the 2015/16 Poetry Society Stanza competition.

'Alteration' and 'Banshee' were first published in *Giant in the Doorway* (Happen*Stance* Press 2012). The pamphlet tells the story of a child struggling to make sense of her mother's psychiatric illness.

I would like to thank, Mimi Khalvati, John McCullough and Catherine Smith for their teaching and inspiration. I'm also grateful to Helena Nelson for her unstinting support and encouragement.

for my daughters

I

Stones

He hears a sound, plip plop. It's small stones thrown
or wet insects on glass. The noise is getting bigger.
It sounds as if stones are being shovelled onto the house.
He asks his cousin if she's experienced anything like this.

He frowns when she says, *It must be possums.*
He smiles when his neighbour says, *Perhaps it's like
when my wife left me.* He laughs when his wife says
Yes, I've been hearing it for a while, it's like memories of home.

He looks up through the leaves of the tree.
Stones are coming down through the branches.
Stones are bouncing off each branch in turn.
Stones are plums falling down like blue stars.

His neighbour looks and says, *Who can be responsible?
Is it the work of clever children?* His cousin gasps and says
Is it the work of aliens, these bright disks as they fall?
Is it, asks his wife, *all the words that need saying?*

In the room, the stones are all over the bed.
The stones are all over the rug but there's no holes
in the ceiling. He looks up and there's no footprints on the roof.
The stones are raining down and he asks his cousin

Why do the stones not fall straight down but seem to turn in the air?
He asks his neighbour, *Why do the stones have no shadow?
Why do the stones fall on my house and not on yours?*
Why, laughs his wife, *it's all the stones that ever got stuck in my shoe.*

Mayan Sacrifice

When we were still together,
we watched a DVD about lost civilisations.
No actors, just temple camera shots

and a presenter talking at the top of the steps.
The corpse, naked, still alive
and painted blue, climbed the same stone steps

(must've been drugged, we agreed)
beat out its heart blood into the butcher's hands
was flung back down the steps to be flayed

(we both leant forward to hear the bounce)
then an ill-fitting blue coat, a second skin
was flapping on the dripping shoulders

of another man (or a woman) dancing
in triumph – something about needing
a death to make things happen.

We both grabbed for the remote but
couldn't find it. He wanted to rewind to
the red hands and the heart's last gasp.

I just needed a moment to pause
(at the bottom of the steps)
to admire my new blue skin.

Young girl with a tree in her brain

Her tree is a rooted scream. She's shown
the lit up neuronets. Coloured lights on the screen

shift and glow, her intimate knowledge branching
out into hungry leaves and buds. She learns

the idea of the object causes the same interference
to the pattern as seeing the object itself. She remembers

his shout in the playground. A grown up once told
her the self is intangible: you cannot

touch the self. But she starts to realise
sometimes her mind can control the shapes

on the screen, can switch and arouse
the lights on and off, so she thinks

maybe, one day, in the same way
she might let him, or not let him.

Virtual

She copies one of the blurry shapes
in her head and makes

a house from a square,
a front door and four windows.

Shopping on her own, she chooses
the right curtains and fills the box

with furniture, lines the furry animals
up on the bed.

He appears smiling and walks around.
He's tall with black hair.

He talks to her in the kitchen, throws
a ball for the dog. One of the children

screams and refuses to eat properly.
The cat dies. There's gunfire in the street.

The car won't start. Someone is knocking
on the door. She switches off the screen

but the noises are getting louder.
The picture folds up.

Somewhere a child is crying.

The Beginning

It was a place he used to think about, the beginning
of a walkway, a glimpse from the getaway car

a corner of a concrete pier, a straggle
of fireweed under a motorway bridge

a one step forward, two steps back place
a scatter of glass on the tarmac. A whisper

saying, *If you recognise this place, it must
already belong to you.* The unloved

places of your body, the back of a knee
the back of your throat, the small of a back.

He was walking unobserved in that place
slippery with leaves after rain

afraid of falling, watching his steps.
A just don't even go there place.

A what were you thinking place.
If he knew who he would meet one day in that place.

Alien

Ryan's in the front room deleting his *Lips of an Angel* ring tone.
A news flash on the TV, a river's in flood on the other side

of the world. An old woman is up to her neck in rushing water.
In panic, she reaches out a hand to grab the overhanging branch

of a tree and looks straight up into the camera. As Ryan notices
her, their eyes meet, a bolt of lightning comes out of nowhere

and her hand slips out of the river, over the wire
into the back of a lorry, onto a boat, into a train

and straight through the TV screen, the rest of the arm
and her body following. Dad looks up from adjusting the iron

to Delicates and hearing a gasp, turns to find out what
it means .He can't see anything but then, like reading words

written in invisible ink, her outline starts to appear
and she slides into the room through a crack in the universe.

At first, she's just a flicker refracted behind bars of shadow
and light, like under water. So Dad says, *What's that*

over there? Is it a hologram or a hoax? If it's a film
in 3-D, then where's the glasses? Nana, who dropped by

to borrow Carly's copy of Twilight, says,
You don't wear glasses, you're too vain, but I see

what you mean it doesn't look human. It's a bad fairy
come to curse us and she waves her stick in the air.

Carly, doing her lip gloss, puts down her mirror
and she's like, *Are you blind? She's a real person*

like me, let's just see what she does. So they all stare
at the woman dripping onto the rug who stares right back

and, for a moment, they all look just like each other.
Then she screams and puts her face up close to the screen

searching for the river, but now there's a cartoon
of a mouse being chased by a cat, so she turns

around and opens her mouth to speak but Mu
(like in an advert) back from her shift at the hospital

with pizza for their tea, not realising that the woman
shouldn't be there, walks into the room and shakes her hand.

Mum says, *Carly, What are you like! Fetch a hair drier
for Nana's friend. Ryan get the plates.* At her touch

the spell breaks and the woman runs out the door
and down the street, disappearing from sight.

As Nana tweets later, *It was a case of ships that pass
in the night, a bat out of hell that vanishes with the light.*

Human

Have you ever experienced any of the following?

    sensation of another presence in the room?

    seeing a bright light in the sky? (yellow doesn't count)

    loss of memory for an hour or more?

    paralysis while something takes off your clothes?

    knowledge that you've been chosen to save humanity?

    body elevation and flight?

    a spiral object inside your right nostril?

    fears of destruction or catastrophe?

    a feeling of being watched much of the time?

    sight of your future alien babies in their cots?

    oneness with God/Nature/The Universe?

    dreaming of a better self?

    puzzling scars on your body?

    a desire to be special?

If you answered Yes to 10 or more questions:

Congratulations you're human!

Grammatical second person talks back

Had it up to here with being You, everyone
wants a piece of me, writing about me, giving
instructions. It's, you do this, you think this
you do that, you feel this, so over it with
epiphanies, swallowing ego is becoming
increasingly uncomfortable, not as authentic
as in my youth. After years of angst, my amygdala
is like a whore's whatsit, if you get my meaning.
Guess it's been a full life, travelled a bit, but time
to put all that behind me, go into recovery
get a few people off my back – find my own glass
slipper, swan in my duckling, flesh in my wooden
puppet moment – no forwarding address.
Tried cloning myself, franchising the concept but
success just meant more meetings. So here's
a substitute for you to interview, maybe not totally
satisfactory, not as inclusive as me, less likely
to be mistaken for fiction, not much presence
very short, but from my point of view, it likes to be
first to take its clothes off in public and that's
the person spec in a nutshell.

How does the body lie?

      How does the body lie?
Like a bird, into a rage, with a dream.

      How does the body fly?
In the dust, in the dress, in the bone.

      How does the body lie?
One day, too soon, one day.

      How does the body die?
On the right, on the back, on the left.

      How does the body lie?
Gut weeps, skin weeps, anus weeps.

      How does the body cry?
With the stars, north to south, in a sleep.

      How does the body lie?
With words, with flesh, with mouths.

Lady Macbeth

She sees her name everywhere in letters
bigger than herself.

> *Like butterflies, he tastes her with his feet.*

She feels naked – a light bulb dangling.

> *He lifts her to his ear, listens for the high pitched*
> *ping which shows she's broken.*

What she wants is a man on a ladder
able to change her, ready to quieten the alarm bell's toll
the knocking on the door.

> *His head, without the crown*
> *weighs just about the same*
> *as a hand held fire extinguisher.*

She thinks she must've been very bad in a previous life.

> *He reads her in bed with a small halogen torch.*

She finds herself unable to stop washing her hands.
Is this wrong.

Malvolio

He's wrong in so many different ways.
Wanting to step up.

Believing what he longs to hear.
Too yellow.

A creature with many places
to fall down into.

Cross-gart'd under sticks.
Smiling inside the mower.

Hibernating in a sack
of turnips. Penned in.

He's hooded, mutilated,
emptied out, set on fire.

And there's the way he howls,
I say to you this house is dark.

As if he knows what he's talking about.
As if he speaks for us all.

Pictures placed on high shelves in hospitals

are probably not there for passing giraffes
to flutter their absurd eyelashes at.
It's more a case of running to catch sight
of something as it's falling.
Maybe they're pictures of you in various stages of undress
in pieces like now. Messages way above my head
I'm not supposed to understand, like x loves y
or the word eternity traced on the beach
with a stick and us underneath as figures in a landscape
the colours weeping.

You're telling me about how you've placed a tiny picture
 of a princess in a ruff, her plain horse face
Tudor airbrushed, on a high shelf as a hidden target
 to verify claims about life after death.
If any out-of-body floating past should view the picture
and remember it, reality will change forever.
And I'm like, shouldn't the pictures be bigger, and then
you're climbing the ladder like a tree, holding a handful
of still life with a cabbage and a quince on strings in front
of a black void and you reach out too far
and learn the hard way the human mind is unreachable.

You fall and I'm running but I can't catch you and the pictures
still in your arms fall apart.
There's a cucumber and a melon cut open on a windowsill,
the seeds so life like as to tempt a passing bird
to peck them and I'm in pieces too, searching for you, thinking
that you're not in the picture
anymore or it's changing because you're looking at it.

Then I'm very afraid because I find you lifeless, on the bed
under a fallen landscape in a huge golden frame
made to show young men a world where docile pink light
is settling on mountains and lakes,

the natives are friendly, it's very new
and the jungle so pretty the temptation is just
to up sticks and go see the view for yourself
and the beasts with such improbable bodies.

Circular Breathing

I'm looking up rebirthing online, how to do it
best and I bump into a man with a beard

on You Tube. He's breathing in circles demonstrating
how to do it, like a prince in a fairy tale trying so hard

to be the best at the test, wanting to win someone special
to love. He breathes down the tube of a straw

into a glass full of pink water. Bubbles rise up like spirits.
I watch the man with the beard gasp, his chest lifts from time

to time and I wonder is he doing it right? The trick is to do it
out of the mouth and in through the nose like giving yourself

a huge kiss under water. I'm very attracted to men who offer me
the key to superior powers, the same thing again and again.

I've been holding my breath my whole life, so I say
to myself, how hard can it be and reach for the kitchen tap.

Immediately, I feel quite light headed as I puff out my cheeks,
an odd feeling, as bubbles rise up, of being in a house with

something missing and also of something being there
which shouldn't and a memory bubbles up of me being

taken to a service where a medium called for someone,
with a name beginning with M, to put their hand up

because she was getting a message from the spirit of a child
who was concerned about a missing watch and I was just

about to put my hand up but before I could she said it must
be a key and a woman wearing a wig in the third row

gasps and says was it maybe her husband who had passed
because the key to her kitchen door went missing the day

of his funeral and the medium said yes it was.
So I was disappointed, like that time I knelt by my bed

doing my best to make myself speak in tongues
but nothing came out and the lady looked superior

as we filed out, as if she'd won something. The music
was rising and falling with a faint bump in the sound.

Air in the cheeks is changing to air in the lungs and I see a pink
face with puffed out cheeks, pressed to the open kitchen window

blowing and sucking at once, playing it like a musical instrument.
Cups and saucers are tinkling and knocking into each other

glasses are moving across the table, the key falls out of the door
onto the floor and I'm quite beside myself, trying so hard to be

special enough to breathe the human spirit into life, that I start
to hyperventilate and faint instead onto the floor and then

I come round and that is when, I see the man with the beard
kneeling beside me with concern, his breath on my face like a kiss.

Blog of the Ninth Lady, Stanton Moor

Things I like about being a stone

I get to spend a lot of time with my circle of friends.
I can keep an eye on Martin the fiddler
and my best friend, Jane Wainwright, see
they don't get up to their old tricks.
Us all sleeping with each other.
This yellow lichen on me because it's the colour
of the petticoat I was wearing
the night I was punished for dancing around being happy.

Things I can't stand

Being awake at 3 a.m. without a drink in my hand.
People I don't like the look of who kiss me
and think that it means something.
Being pissed up against.
How tight it is in here.
When I wake up from a dream about my mother
and everything still looks the same.
The time a young man came up behind me
and touched my back
just gently
and me not being able to turn around and say:
Do that again, please do that to me again.

II

The Dreamer

Traffic

A distant repetition of height
and collapse.

She's hanging a mirror in every room
for visitors mainly.

It's too early for coast road traffic, the pause
of lorries changing down on the hill.

Is it water taller than her she can hear
turning itself inside out

or a queue of taxis back from the clubs
too far gone? Not to know for sure.

Threading a needle in the dark
all fingers and thumbs.

The Sleeper

What can she see behind her eyelids,
is it rapid skies, galaxies on fire?

Can she hear voices on the other side
of the ward, our footsteps

light and fearful?
With folded arms and a puzzled

frown, how distant
she looks, moving away from us

as if she were a bird,
asleep on the wing,

half of her brain shut down,
or a child of spacemen travelling

for generations unable to remember
what she was trying to find.

Snowing

Even when she's out of the room,
or asleep, she can feel the trembling

of sheets flung to the floor,
of rings she dropped to let in more air.

It's bad luck to guess another person's dreams
but what if it really had been snowing

across the bed and she descending,
as a blaze of white, a mirage,

a hand in front of her lips to shelter
the words coming in and out in waves

of astonishment. Her mouth working,
eating itself, like walking slowly downstairs.

Fetch

Her body sleeps on in bed
while outside, she walks home at midnight.

She feels her rapid heart beat against
the pavement, the count of lamp posts,

dreams her own footsteps across the bed.
She starts as if awake and greets herself

as supplicant, standing key in hand,
anxious to be inside. The feather of her kiss.

The sleepers folding up, unfolding.

Chicken

She must like it or else she'd stop.
She thinks the coast road is her own bed.

She doesn't know how to make it stop.
If anyone goes to help, she's a dog in a river,

they jump in, they drown. She scrambles out
woofing on the other side. All the thanks they get.

She's done it before, has she done it before.
Faces in the long coach skitter past

crouched smaller, the lights not easy to see.
Someone lies awake beside her.

Is someone lying awake beside her
trying to cross, the invisible sea pulling?

Dusk

She's started to avoid mirrors again.
They make other people's faces seem
bigger than they should be

and sometimes much nearer.
Perhaps 'mirror' is really another word
for the idea of night

as if the glass, like a leaf, might curl
and drop, leaving only a frame
where the day was.

There would be a fold inside her then,
a trace of water in the air, flying insects.
But, in truth, the many absences

of night need never be complete,
in a forest or in a story,
if a bargain with the dark can be struck.

La mer

There's something horrifying about the sea.
Up close, it's like a mother, moody,
often in pieces and almost never tender.
It's right up there, in terms of remorseless
beauty, with moon, stars, heart. I feel a kind
of guilt that I didn't stay closer to the sea,
as she was drowning, her frantic folding
and unfolding hands of bird and sky.
I lie in bed and remember her gasp
and stutter, her uncertain shifting light.
From a distance, horizons of stared
at water reaching up into air,
might easily be misunderstood
as soft to touch, welcoming as flesh.

Normality

Yes, it is impossible to find changeless water.
Water will raise no boundary
but take the character of sky or gold
or blood, bearing in stained and long
shaking fingers, the impress
of flapping black wings:
migratory birds.

Change by self division causes abnormality
into ice and water,
or Medusean fields of solid green scum,
as water self aware
changes from within.

But you are normal, quick shifting, thoughtless:
my envied daughter.

Oil Spill

The sea is on fire with many traces
of death the birds won't fly over.

She glimpses another life in flashbacks.
Layers of oil float on the surface, collude

to prevent light entering the water.
But, there is no surface, only many centres.

She was tricked into looking in the wrong direction,
a bird wearing a coat of oil, mantling

with spread wings, fanning out a slick black tail,
arched over water, vulnerable to dispersion.

This is the seduction of light, how everyone,
in moments of weakness, hands spilling out,

glimpses another life in flashbacks
(is tricked into looking in the wrong direction)

is drawn to it, wants to touch it.
She wakes and dreams fly up

from the centre like cleansed birds.
But, there is no centre, only

many surfaces, with traces of death,
hands spilling out, drawn to it, wanting to touch it.

Banshee

has a booking for a death,
warns and wails in frantic bursts
unable to handkerchief herself
flings down water onto her naked hair

throws herself across the landscape
howls and howls
calls out with a broken voice
spits leaves into the air.

At midnight, she takes off her make up
washes and blow dries her hair
admires herself in the mirror
drops her comb.

A woman with red eyes
and something screaming in her head
comes into the bathroom for a glass of water
picks up the comb

then falls like a knight from a horse.
Between stirrup and ground,
banshee spirits her away
won't let my mother change her mind

won't let her spit the tablets back into the box
won't let her reach upwards
in slow motion, to grasp and ride again
her own warm body breathing.

Full Hunger Moon

Full snow moon
undresses
on a chilly night
two white bodies
dancing
in our birthday suits.

Dark moon
        hides herself
behind the sun.
I look where
        she was sleeping
and she's not there.

Full hunger moon is very thin. I can't get near to touch her.

Wolf moon
is laughing.
Her teeth
are big as snow.

Full crust moon
trembles in latex gloves
        freezes and thaws
thaws and freezes.

Hearing Voices

We just wanted to be noticed,
to be nearer to her than anyone,

had no learning or grace,
busied ourselves putting words under her tongue,

told her what she was afraid to hear,
made her repeat it.

Lifted our arms to be picked up,
cried out for her in the night,

couldn't think what to do
when she raged at coats left untidy in the hall.

Looked at the way she had of trembling and knew
she wasn't quite right, knew she wasn't family.

The Wreath

She makes it from parts of herself,
a last breath, a collar bone,
the troubled voices. Death replies

by knotting together the Thief,
the Trumpet and the Stopper.
With a round turn and two half hitches,

I tie it to the mast. Aloft
in a sea of lamentation,
extravagant weeping and apology,

held but not healed, grief
is a world fixed at three points, The Above
The Below and the Winged Creature.

Alteration

1.

I have her skull and some soft tissue
in the museum. I use
3D software, a slap of clay.

The head is much admired
until eye sockets weep rusty blood
and milk. I cross myself

pull it down with ropes. Knock
half her nose off. Pin her to a wall.
Install it. The label reads

Body part – Unknown.

2.

I choose a new face for her.
I see it in a shop window,
dream of it, save up my change.

It hangs with a beauty I always
wanted for her.
How she must really be inside.

She has a left side
which is a perfect copy of the right.
She has open ears and full lips.

She lets her smile fall up into her eyes.
She doesn't break eye contact, almost like
she knows who I am.

III

Recognition

I'm walking past all the faces and you see me
as less, no song but just a word in passing.

She wants to make your feet quicken
as you sense her loud fierce pace behind.

I'm a cloud seen through a window and forgotten
as I shrink out of the corner of your eye.

She wants her name in lights and a shadow
to shatter the shop windows up and down the street.

I'm sure you turn to look, but I see you do not
change, as you hear my step behind.

She wants to be the lamp that warns of danger
that sweeps hot light across your eyes.

I'm watching as you walk up behind her
to lift the mask from her face.

She turns and cries out with love
as I see, in my dream, that you know me.

Living Statues

1.

My best friend lives inside a small green tent.
It's got a face grid like on a burqa.
Sometimes she reminds me of my mother.

She plays jingly music to attract
the kids. She has no front door but
just a slit from which she wiggles

two silver fingers in a comical fashion.
I don't have to finish my sentences when she's around.
She can't see how much money is in the hat.

2.

The friend I always wished for is never lonely.
She wears a reptilian blue and silver mask
with no eyes, silver body paint and not a lot else

although it's chilly in the wind by the river.
She gives out just exactly the right amount
of herself to everyone she meets.

Her bike isn't real. She pedals vigorously
and makes the wheels hum when she hears
a coin clink in the bowl.

3.

The friend I would like to become has
lost her head. It's sunk inside her silver ruff.
She keeps absolutely still.

She's squat and dignified and doesn't talk
about herself too much. She's got no hat.
Her costume is complicated with layers

of petticoats and lines of pearls.
Just when I get really tired of staring at her
she lifts one hand but very slowly.

Nest
'Show me your hands if we be friends' Shakespeare

Is the shock of discovery,
the urge to touch and not to touch

to look inside.
It has no weight in the hand.

In a cleft between two limbs,
it's light as an opening to another world.

A room deep inside
(metaphor is a kind of shyness)

impossible to reach,
it's like a hand itself

private and empty.
Show me your hands.

Blind Mirror
(installed at Tate Modern)

Inside an oblong frame, unlit blue
isn't water or sky or distance.

It's a layer of spongy plasticine
smeared and pitted by the impression

of many faces pushed into it so
I shut my eyes and pretending to be blind

lift my face into the clammy looking-glass.
It's like kissing a wet fish.

On one of the black leather sofas, blocking the view
two Goths are stretched out with loved-up smiles

their eyes and limbs stuck together.
No one is sitting next to them.

Planet earth has shrunk to hold just two
and I think how eyes need to move, seek

other eyes out, create invisible
lines of touch and I wonder how it might

feel, to have only a dim plastic shape
to dare offer up a hesitant face to.

Hotel Room

Are you the person I'm expecting to meet?
In the bathroom mirror, other people's faces cover mine.

Silence is making this spaceship seem larger.
I can hear someone moving the furniture around, is it me?

In the bathroom mirror, other people's faces cover mine.
I can't help dreaming of home light years away.

I can hear someone moving the furniture around, is it me?
Energetic Chinese voices from next door, the sound of splashing.

I can't help dreaming of home light years away.
If we are most ourselves when unobserved.

Energetic Chinese voices from next door, the sound of splashing.
There's a smell of fresh paint, someone's hair in the waste bin.

If we are most ourselves when unobserved.
I can feel my heart beating.

There's a smell of fresh paint, someone's hair in the waste bin.
Hanging, motionless, above the body in the bed,

I can feel my heart beating.
Silence is making this space ship seem larger.

Hanging, motionless, above the body in the bed,
are you the person I'm expecting to meet?

The Misadventures of Her Purse

Picaresque and pert, easy at first, it was made
of red faux leather with a gilt clasp of two curved

metal halves which clicked open and shut,
identical twins: two swans necking like Beauty

and Terror. But she left it, forgotten, inside
a paper bag from the buffet on Virgin Express,

along with a Kit Kat wrapper, an empty
coffee cup and a packet of wet wipes. Losing

her money and cards, she felt a strange lightness
like the burden of a self lifted. After its recovery

from Lost Property, it was stolen as she ordered
five Pimms at the bar and she wished it had

been equipped with an alarm to wake her at 4 am
with its screams and the sounds and lights of two

police cars and a police van. She wondered who
or what had touched it after her, imagining mirror,

lipstick, pieces of paper, being tossed out into
the wind in the wrong direction, like human ashes

scattered somewhere beautiful, perhaps under
trees beside a river where swans dip and feed,

and flying back into an unknown face.
Its reincarnation was in the form of white plastic

with a golden zip. It became hidden under a giant
pack of kitchen roll in a Lidl basket and, along

with her shopping, was left at the checkout, when
she had a last minute wobble about the purchase

of a three bird roast, one inside the other.
The purse lay in the basket, Moses in the rushes,

becoming increasingly anxious until the joy
of its owner's return. Newly awakened to wisdom

and made self conscious by suffering, it developed
the ability to topple objects like a poltergeist.

She emptied her handbag onto the car roof
looking for her keys and, distracted by a wasp,

left the purse there so it found itself jolting along
the M25 in the direction of Gatwick. Whereupon,

taking wing, it flew with all the destructive
passion it could muster and landed in the central

reservation. Impossible for her to retrieve,
the purse lay for days, weeks, months, without

rescue. Afraid of its ability to cause grief to others,
at the end, it was grateful for its fading into debris,

an obsessive undercurrent in a dream, a plastic
glimmer of white feathers now open, now shut.

Moths

rain down shadows bigger than the lamp
      bigger than New York.

Shaking against the wall, they cast themselves
      into rabbit or dog or witch.

Moths push forward forever. They don't
      understand how she feels, won't
let her be one of them.

Oh! but the moths are crawling
      through her long hair. They're colliding
with the perfume of her fingers.

I hope they know she wouldn't
      try to harm them. She didn't
mean to stand in front of their light.

Ekphrastic

She's skating with high visibility feet. Not
melting into nature at all.

Most of the men have their backs to her.

Two thirds of the world is frantic with sky.

A small diagonal tree refuses to look.
        A municipal building turns away.
                Sightlines vanish.

Most of the ice is faintly pink.
        The pressure of her blood is low.
                A boat tilts.

A man, wearing a tall black hat, places
his hand on a globe.

He's walking out of the frame.

He's so much better than her.

Mr and Mrs Death

He was always a few millimetres
under her skin, a parallel universe

the same shape as her shape.
She's a bowl of fruit decaying

in a speeded up video installation
collapses with his bruise inside.

His vase is a shaft of no light
her entrance a door opening inwards.

She rises up, to open to the beloved
a conjurer who swallows her own wand.

She sucks pomegranate seeds from his fingers
hopes her mother knows where she is

notices the lock
is choking on the key.

There's no window to look at the security lights from.
She can't see the dogs on the lawn.

Black Ice

It's the idea of it that's so damaging.
    A simple step out of the back door
        feet shoot from under.

You try to remember the shape of standing
    trip over an invisible banana skin
        a cut flower under snow.

You shout out a name!
    Drop too many exclamation marks
        slide into a tree,

can't say what you need
    observe time in slow motion
        damage a river not even slightly.

Out of order, you know it's wrong but fall harder.
    It's not fast or safe
        not held.

Boundaries

are there for a reason what's that all about if you step over
a few you become way
out. of order in a queue of people going round the block
& after a few times
you are in no man's land sitting in a bus shelter in a desert
in an advert
next to a sign post which says 600km to dialysis or something
like that to make
a point. about the spaces. between people & you don't want
to be a loser
all your life so you try to step back over the line running
under the landscape
will have shifted so you are looking at yourself in a mirror
texting a message
on a bike in a gym & flicking a paperback on how Now
is all you've got &
how to become your best self & recover like a river after drought
& the line of the river
on the TV news on the wall becomes a flood. no short cuts.
across the landscape
& people clinging to trees at the bank cars floating
& the voices too far away to hear & you end. up washed up
in your neighbour's garden
in his face again & on the face of it that must mean the line
found you thinking
that the story you are living in about now needs to breathe. speed
up some more
before it stops. you step over it again & seems like
it's all over
the place so there's no place to go so you say to yourself
get a grip & you just
want to say to yourself this ends. here this ends. here now.
this ends here. now.

Sense of everything

The air is broken by a body moving in the night
people are staying inside their houses

what I'm most afraid of is the possibility of noises in the wall
she's face down breathing the shallow air below the smoke

his house is under surveillance
a lonely tower with a red hood and a tiny door

there's a photo of a face in the priest hole
each body part disappears in turn

impossible to predict we would be unable to make sense of everything

only to reappear as things, your eye is in the kitchen sink
his finger with the gold ring was on the mat

he's hiding from the people
running up and down the corridors, not able

to remember that elusive moment just before you fall asleep
like pushing open a door

which she thought would be heavy and falling forward
when it turns out to be light

On the last day

As the sky burns, graves crack open
and bodies rise victorious, you'll be heaving
your 23 kilos into the boot of a taxi.

The last word will be uttered, as bones reassemble,
not by someone you love, but by that weird bloke
at the club, who made those remarks about your bladder.

Cycling past, he'll shout, *See you Friday, bring a fiver
for the quiz nite.* Or even worse, in the security queue
at the airport, if you make the mistake of looking back,

you'll see, among the angels and the shafts of light,
someone you only half remember, making
incoherent foot movements in the dust:

dancing out directions like a bee.
Then, just as you begin to understand which way to go,
the bomb making residue man will call you over

to open your bag to be checked and the meaning
of it all will fall, along with seven tampons, a wreath
of flowers, three unidentifiable white tablets and a pair

of manicure scissors right out of the carry on bag
of your head and that's probably what will happen
on the last day or the one after that.

The Spoiler

He's running towards her with the ending in his hand.
        The audience flick off screens

pretend to be shop dummies,
        stand quaking in door frames.

His figure is tall as a block of flats,
        the next minute, tiny as a button.

Cities give him their freedom quickly.
        Trees form into circles for their own protection.

Street lamps switch on and off and weep.
        He's still clutching the piece of paper,

now in his hat like a feather,
        now in his shoe as a plaster.

Shrugging snow from his coat,
        he turns right, up the stairs, along the corridor,

five chandeliers gang together, rain down
        mirrors without faces.

He stumbles forward wiping his eyes.
        Bits of the journey are falling off in handfuls.

He calls out her name, rehearses his message,
        limps across the lobby.

Is it a heart attack, an avalanche or a kiss?
        She shakes against the wall paper.

Lightning Source UK Ltd.
Milton Keynes UK
UKOW06f0338060216

267834UK00002BA/24/P

9 781848 614956